ON THE ROAD TO EMMAUS

ON THE ROAD TO EMMAUS
Eucharistic Renewal Today
Bishop Donal Murray

VERITAS

First published 1990
Revised and updated 2011
Veritas Publications
7–8 Lower Abbey Street
Dublin 1
Ireland
publications@veritas.ie
www.veritas.ie

ISBN 978 1 84730 318 9

Copyright © Bishop Donal Murray, 2011

The material in this publication is protected by copyright law. Except as may be permitted by law, no part of the material may be reproduced (including by storage in a retrieval system) or transmitted in any form or by any means, adapted, rented or lent without the written permission of the copyright owners. Applications for permissions should be addressed to the publisher.

A catalogue record for this book is available from the British Library.

Designed by Shane Dunne, Veritas
Printed in the Republic of Ireland by Turners Printing Company Limited, Longford

Veritas books are printed on paper made from the wood pulp of managed forests. For every tree felled, at least one tree is planted, thereby renewing natural resources.

Introduction

On 29 September 1979, for the first time in history, a Pope celebrated the Eucharist in Ireland. On that occasion Blessed John Paul II said: 'We are one in faith and spirit with the vast throng which filled this Phoenix Park on the occasion of the last great Eucharistic hosting held on this spot, at the Eucharistic Congress in 1932.'[1] As we recall those two great events, it is good to reflect on the Eucharist and on what it should mean to us.

The Gospel account of the disciples on the road to Emmaus (Luke 24:13-35) will provide a focus for our reflections.[2]

Our own hope had been ... (v. 21)

It is not hard for us to sympathise with the disillusioned disciples. Our hopes had been that our country would continue to take her place among the nations of the earth, playing an increasingly positive role in the world, with a respected role in the United Nations and the European Union, with prosperity and well-being of all the children of the nation. We hoped that Ireland would continue to play an important role in the missionary outreach of the Church and that the faith of Ireland would remain strong.

We have seen instead an economy in ruins, unemployment and recession worse than that which faced us as we entered the 1980s. We have also seen the decline of the Church in terms of all the statistics of religious practice, of vocations and of belief. We have recognised that for some the Church has been a source of unspeakable pain, above all for those whose lives have been so

---

1. All passages in quotation marks and indented paragraphs, unless otherwise indicated, are from the homily of Blessed John Paul in the Phoenix Park on 29 September 1979.
2. All Scripture quotations, unless otherwise indicated, are taken from the Jerusalem Bible.

cruelly blighted by child sexual abuse. In these and many other ways we can say 'Our hope had been …'

Hope can be lost in two ways. The first is to place one's hope in things that cannot sustain it. Pope John Paul was concerned to alert us to how easily that can happen.

We are, he pointed out, surrounded by 'values and trends that up to now have been alien to Irish society … pervading materialism imposes its dominion … in many different forms and with an aggressiveness that spares no one.'

This was not a call to retreat into nostalgic isolationism. No one was more insistent than Pope John Paul on the need to be outward-looking, on the need to go out to bring the Gospel to the world, and in particular to the western world. The point he was making, and the point which is even more pressing today, is of the need to strengthen our own faith and to be more deeply convinced of the light which it can bring to the world.

It is no accident that the Pope chose to focus his time in Dublin on the Eucharist. The influence of materialism and consumerism is first felt in the capital city. Here can be seen most clearly the contrasts of wealth and poverty, the gods of success and affluence and status, the temptation to lose sight of human and Christian values. In our day, we might add that Dublin was the centre of the housing boom, and of the banks and financial services which were at the heart of the collapse.

Every modern city suffers such challenges. 'Many people,' Pope John Paul said, 'are tempted to self-indulgence and consumerism … human identity is defined by what one owns. The challenge that is already with us is the temptation to accept as true freedom what is in reality only a new form of slavery.' These challenges are not, of course, confined to the city. In the intervening years they spread to every part of the country and, as we know to our cost, have borne fruit in economic collapse and social problems of many kinds.

In the Irish tradition of faithfulness to the Eucharist there lies the hope of keeping a true perspective on these temptations:

And so, it becomes all the more urgent to steep ourselves in the truth that comes from Christ, 'who is the way, the truth and the life', and in the strength that he himself offers us through his Spirit. It is especially in the Eucharist that the power and love of the Lord are given to us.

In the Eucharist, the truth that comes from Christ is crystallised for us. There we recognise most clearly where our hope lies. We are not defined by what we own but by what we are. And what we are is a people saved in Christ.

In the Mass, we are in the presence of the moment of truth that gives meaning to the whole of human history. Christ is present to us in the very act of offering himself to his Father. He is present in the act of supreme love that is 'his great victory over sin and death – a victory he communicates to us'. Only in the truth that comes from Christ, the truth that *is* Christ, can one regard human life with a hope that can look death and evil in the face. This is the truth, the only truth 'that makes us free' (Jn 8:32, NEW REVISED STANDARD VERSION).

Anyone who seeks to place his or her hope elsewhere is enslaved. We become slaves when we place our hope in things that have no power to give us real happiness. We become slaves when we define ourselves, or allow ourselves to be defined, by what we own, by our status, by our popularity, rather than by what we are. We become slaves to what is only illusory, like the idolaters mocked by the psalmist: 'Their idols are silver and gold, the work of human hands. They have mouths but do not speak, eyes but do not see, ears but do not hear … Those who make them are like them; so are all who trust in them' (Ps 115:4, 5, 8, NRSV).

That is why we need to steep ourselves in the truth that comes from Christ. The Mass is not just a reminder but a *making present* of the victory over sin and death which is communicated to us and which makes us free. Everything that can diminish us, everything that can divide us, everything that can destroy us, *is overcome*. The optimism of the 1960s, expressed in song, 'We shall overcome,' fell short of the reality of Christian hope. Christ has already overcome. We are a people saved in Christ and offered a share in his victory and his glory. There lies the real freedom.

In the light of that truth made present in the Eucharist, we get a new perspective on the things that consumerism and materialism offer as sources of human happiness. Their emptiness, when they are treated as though they could provide the meaning of life, becomes clear. Happiness does not lie in wealth or in power or in social standing. Happiness is much more than any of that: it is freedom from evil and death in the glorious life of the Son of the infinite God. The Lord made us and redeemed us for that life – and our hearts, as St Augustine said, are restless until they rest in him. Beside that, all other truths are secondary. We are children of God, made to be like him and to see him as he is (1 Jn 3:2). 'The sacrifice of the Mass,' Pope John Paul said in the Park, 'is meant to be the festive celebration of our salvation.'

The truth that we are celebrating is so profound that it gives rise to wonder at ourselves and to adoration of God: 'In reality, the name for that deep amazement at human worth and dignity is the Gospel ... It is also called Christianity.'[3] In the Mass, Irish people down the centuries have found 'the spiritual strength to live, even through times of greatest hardship and poverty, through days of persecutions and vexations ... The Eucharist transformed their souls for eternal life, in union with the living God.'

Hope can also be weakened or lost in another way. Even in a person who remains convinced that the truth of Christ, and it alone, can set us free, the conviction can weaken through lack of reflection and prayer. Although we would be horrified to be accused of not having Christ at the centre of our lives, we very rarely stop to tell him so. Our lives are lived always on the surface; ultimate questions are quietly ignored.

The strange thing about human beings is that we can lose our grip on what we know to be of fundamental importance

---

3. John Paul II, *Redemptor Hominis*, 10.

because we allow ourselves to become absorbed by the 'urgency' of things that we know in our hearts to be trivial. Even the 'deep amazement' of the Good News may be dissipated if one never thinks about it.

Has there ever before been a culture in which there was so little opportunity for reflection? Every silence is filled with sound, every wandering attention is grabbed by somebody trying to sell something, even leisure is 'laid on' and piped into one's home.

The Sunday Mass is an all too brief change of tempo. It too can easily be infected by the fear of silence and by the drive for speed and efficiency. Even when the celebration is of excellent quality, the change of focus to reflect on ultimate questions and on the profound truth that makes us free is not easily achieved.

We need, the Holy Father said, to steep ourselves in the truth that comes from Christ. The word 'steep' is well chosen. We need to immerse ourselves in that truth again and again, day by day. If not, like potted plants we all too quickly begin to dry out and die. If the truth does not 'sink in' and change us, it remains unable to affect us and we can remain untouched. The disciples on the road to Emmaus had heard that some women had come back from the tomb saying that it was empty and that angels had told them that Jesus had risen (Lk 24:21-23). The message had left them untouched!

That is why Pope Paul VI saw the need to insist 'time and time again on the need for baptised Christians to be faithful to the Sunday celebration, in joy, of the Eucharist … This is the culmination on earth of the covenant of love between God and his people: the sign and source of Christian joy, the preparation for the eternal feast.'[4]

Only if we are steeped in the knowledge of our calling in Christ can we recognise false, counterfeit freedoms for the shallow illusions that they are. Only if we live in 'deep amazement' at the Good News will it enlighten and transform our whole lives. In the Eucharist we

---

4. Paul VI, *Gaudete in Domino*, Conclusion.

celebrate who we really are – people saved in Christ, passing with him into a new life beyond death and evil and suffering, people filled with the Holy Spirit, the giver of life, people giving thanks to God our Father. That, after all, is what the word 'Eucharist' means – thanksgiving.

And their eyes were opened ... (v. 31)

One of the complaints sometimes made, especially by young people, is that those who are regular Massgoers do not seem to live very Christian lives. No doubt that complaint may frequently fail to take into account how demanding a truly Christian life can be and how dishearteningly often a person's best efforts may fall short.

At the same time, the complaint expresses a real insight. Our participation in the Eucharist ought to change our lives. 'Our union with Christ in the Eucharist must be expressed in the truth of our lives today.'

That means that our lives must be based on the real truth about human life and destiny. We find the truth in the selfless love of Christ, giving himself up to agony, mockery, brutality and death out of love for his Father and for us.

We cannot really be steeped in that truth without recognising that our love, such as it is, is half-hearted, timid and calculating by comparison with his: 'precisely because it is without limit, [Christ's] self-giving gives rise in us human beings, subject to numerous limitations, to the need to turn to God in an ever more mature way and with a constant, ever more profound conversion'.[5]

The eyes of the two disciples of Emmaus were opened and they understood what their companion had been saying to them on the road: 'Was it not ordained that the Christ should suffer and so enter into his glory?' (Lk 24:32). He had been explaining to them that, in this sinful world, love has to be sacrificial. Love

---

5. *Redemptor Hominis*, 20.

has to struggle to overcome hatred and ingratitude and selfishness. Really to love means being ready to suffer and to change.

In his first encyclical, published a few months before his visit to Ireland, Blessed John Paul refers to three aspects of the Eucharist – and the first of these is sacrifice: 'It is at one and the same time a Sacrifice-Sacrament, a Communion-Sacrament, and a Presence-Sacrament.'[6]

In the Mass, we are in the presence of Christ's Body, broken and given up for us, and of Christ's Blood, poured out for us in the agony and cruelty of a Roman execution. That becomes the standard by which our love is to be judged:

> The truth of our union with Christ in the Eucharist is tested by whether or not we really love our fellow men and women; it is tested by how we treat others, especially our families … It is tested by whether or not we try to be reconciled to our enemies, or whether or not we forgive those who hurt us or offend us. It is tested by whether we practise in our lives what our faith teaches us.

To participate in the Sacrifice-Sacrament of the Eucharist means being ready to show others the self-sacrificing love of Christ and it means offering ourselves without reservation to his Father with him in his sacrifice.

Sacrifice, in the proper sense of the word, is an act which recognises the supremacy and the sovereignty of God. Whether it is a question of the ancient sacrifices of crops and animals or the Sacrifice of the New Covenant in the Mass, it is, first and foremost, an act of worship, of adoration.

Animals and other valuable possessions were offered in order to acknowledge that all creation, and more particularly the offerers themselves, belonged to God. In the Mass, the Incarnate Word, through whom all things were made, offers himself and the whole created universe to his Father.

---

6. Ibid.

> And so, with all the Powers of heaven,
> we worship you constantly on earth,
> while, with all the Church,
> as one voice we acclaim:
> Holy, Holy, Holy Lord God of hosts.
> Heaven and earth are full of your glory.
> Hosanna in the highest.
> Blessed is he who comes in the name of the Lord.
> Hosanna in the highest.[7]

Taking part in the Mass means gathering up the whole of one's life, and the whole of oneself into that praise and worship of the Father's glory, through, with and in Christ. If it is a genuine participation, it cannot but affect the way in which we see every moment and corner of life. All of us have many interests, activities, attachments and ambitions in which we do not acknowledge and live the faith we proclaim at Mass. There are many ways in which our lives do not recognise the sovereignty and the glory of God.

The Sacrifice-Sacrament of the Eucharist is a call to open our eyes to the real meaning and the real task of the common priesthood of Christ's faithful:

> For all their works, prayers and apostolic undertakings, family and married life, daily works, relaxation of mind and body, if they are accomplished in the Spirit – indeed even the hardships of life is patiently borne – all these become spiritual sacrifices acceptable to God through Jesus Christ (cf. 1 Pet 2:5). In the celebration of the Eucharist these may most fittingly be offered to the Father along with the Body of the Lord. And so, worshipping everywhere by their holy actions, the laity consecrate the world itself to God.[8]

---

7. *Roman Missal*, 2011.
8. Vatican II, *Lumen Gentium*, 34.

To the accusation that we have not allowed our eyes to be opened to that reality, that our lives do not reflect the greatness of our calling, we can only plead guilty. In the Mass, we have been shown who we are in the light of God's love for us. Our lives have not been transformed as they ought by that conviction. We can hope that when our lives are ended, it may be possible to say of us what Pope John Paul said of those who have gone before us: 'The Eucharist transformed their souls for eternal life, in union with the living God.'

He vanished out of their sight (v. 31)

A common thread in the appearances of Jesus after the resurrection is that even his closest disciples failed to recognise him. Mary Magdalene thought he was the gardener (Jn 20:15); only when their nets were breaking with the huge catch of fishes did John say 'It is the Lord!' (Jn 21:7). The disciples on the road to Emmaus also failed to recognise him. As soon as she did recognise him, Mary Magdalene was told not to cling to him; and when the two disciples recognised him, he immediately vanished from their sight.

The Risen Lord is no ghost. He meets his disciples; he eats and drinks with them as he had done in the past. And yet it is different. They are now learning that he is present in a new way. He is closer than ever, but they are not to cling to the kind of relationship they had with him before:

> The Lord sits at table with his disciples as before, with thanks and praise and breaking of bread. Then he vanishes from their outward view, and through this vanishing their outward vision is opened up and they recognise him. It is a real table fellowship, and yet it is new. In the breaking of the bread he manifests himself, yet only in vanishing does he become truly recognisable.[9]

---

9. J. Ratzinger, Benedict XVI, *Jesus of Nazareth, Vol. II: Holy Week*, San Francisco: Ignatius Press, 2011, p. 270.

This is the two-fold truth that the Eucharist makes present. The dimension of our present existence is true and worthwhile. It is here that we meet Christ and walk with him. He is with us as he promised. But we have not here a lasting city. We look to the new creation that Jesus has entered by his death and resurrection – the glory that he had with his Father before the world was made.

We should not cling to this world as if that were all there is. That would mean living as if our ultimate goal could be found in what we have and what we achieve. We would be yielding to the temptation that Jesus firmly rejected at the beginning of his mission, the temptation to put something else – possessions, popularity or power – in the place of God. It is by God's word alone that we live and it is God alone that we must serve (cf. Mt 4:1-11; Lk 4:1-13).

At the same time, just as the Risen Jesus – whose body is no longer subject to the limitations of space and time – is the same Jesus of Nazareth whom they knew, so the new creation is not alien to this world. All that is good and true in our relationships, our achievements, our freedom and enterprise, we will find again:

> ... but freed of stain, burnished and transfigured, when Christ hands over to the Father: 'a kingdom eternal and universal, a kingdom of truth and life, of holiness and grace, of justice, love and peace'. On this earth that Kingdom is already present in mystery. When the Lord returns it will be brought into full flower.[10]

All of this is expressed in the prayers that accompany the presentation of the gifts at Mass. When we offer 'the fruit of the earth and the work of human hands' and when we ask that 'we may be accepted by you, O Lord', we recognise that we and this world are on the way to a new creation which will take us beyond any clinging to what we possess. It will instead open our arms to

---

10. Vatican II, *Gaudium et Spes*, 39.

receive the life which is God's gift, and in which the deepest human longings will be fulfilled beyond all expectation or imagining. We prepare ourselves for that transformation by seeking to make ourselves and all that we have a gift to God. We are destined to share in the divinity of Christ 'who humbled himself to share in our humanity'.

At the breaking of bread (v. 35)

The Eucharist is the standard by which our lives are judged, first of all because it is the celebration of what humanity is called to be in Jesus Christ who is the Way. It is the standard also because the divine love, revealed in the broken Body and the flowing Blood, is a love given to all of us together. 'If we are children we are heirs as well: heirs of God and coheirs with Christ, sharing his sufferings so as to share his glory' (Rom 8:17).

If the almighty Father sees his Son in each person, then we too must see Christ in everyone. Everyone who is baptised is baptised into his Body. We cannot, therefore, worship his Body in the Eucharist without at the same time deepening our union with those who are part of his Body with us.

The Eucharist makes present the Body of Christ and builds up the Body of Christ. The two aspects cannot be divorced. St Augustine suggests that when the priest says, 'The Body of Christ' and a person answers 'Amen', the answer means not just 'I believe that this is the Body of Christ' but also 'I believe that we are the Body of Christ.'[11]

The Eucharist is a Communion-Sacrament. By receiving the Body of Christ, we are transformed into the Body of Christ.

> Communion with the Body of Christ in the Eucharist signifies and brings about, or builds up, the intimate union of all the faithful in the Body of Christ, which is the Church.[12]

---

11. Cf. Augustine Sermon, 272.
12. Synod of Bishops 1985, The Final Report, b, c. 1.

'The "breaking of bread" gave the entire Eucharistic action its name in apostolic times. It signifies that by receiving Communion we are made one body in the bread of life which is Christ' (cf. 1 Corinthians 10:17).[13] The unity among ourselves which we celebrate in the Eucharist is not just our shared interests, our belonging to the same neighbourhood, even our common humanity. It is, more fundamentally, 'our communion with God through Jesus Christ in the Holy Spirit'.[14] It is the communion (*koinonia*) that allows us to join together in prayer to God our common Father, through our one Lord, Jesus Christ, his Son, in the unity of the Holy Spirit.

The more we understand the meaning of that unity, the more we see other human beings as brothers and sisters. We recognise that our sharing in the eternal banquet, which the Eucharist foreshadows, depends on our treatment of all the sons and daughters of God. The union with God for which we hope is a union that we can only enter if we are willing to share it with all who are called by God.

At Mass, the family of God is gathered around his table. Being ready to sit at that table means being ready to love all of them without exception. This was the firm instruction of Christ himself, an instruction that his Church has always thought of in relation to the Eucharist: 'So then, if you are bringing your offering to the altar and there remember that your brother has something against you, leave your offering there before the altar, go and be reconciled with your brother first, and then come back and present your offering' (Mt 5:23, 24).

The meaning of the breaking of bread has concrete, practical implications for our attitude to one another. Pope John Paul said in his message to the International Eucharistic Congress in Lourdes in 1981:

---

13. Cf. *General Instruction on the Roman Missal*, 83.
14. Synod of Bishops 1985, The Final Report, c. 3.

> The Congress has taught you to live the breaking of the bread as Church, according to all its demands: welcoming, exchanging, sharing, going beyond barriers, being concerned for the conversion of people, the renunciation of prejudices, the transforming of our social milieu in structures and spirit. You have understood that to be true and logical your meeting at the Eucharistic table must have practical consequences.[15]

In the liturgy, 'we take part in a foretaste of that heavenly liturgy which is celebrated in the Holy City of Jerusalem toward which we journey as pilgrims, where Christ is sitting at the right hand of God'.[16] In the liturgy, we proclaim that we are waiting 'in joyful hope' for Christ to come again. To be genuine, our prayer must involve the recognition that our attitudes towards our brothers and sisters are not yet those of the eternal kingdom. It must also involve the practical determination to do something about it. Only then have we understood the breaking of bread:

> Really sharing in the body of the Lord in the breaking of the Eucharistic Bread, we are taken up into communion with him and with one another. 'Because the bread is one, we, through many, are one body, all of us who partake of the one bread' (1 Cor 10:17). In this way all of us are made members of his body (cf. 1 Cor 12:27), 'but severally members of one another' (Rom 12:4).[17]

But the Blessed Eucharist is not just the standard against which our lives and attitudes are to be measured, it is also the source of the power to change our lives. This too was part of Pope John Paul's message in Dublin:

---

15. John Paul II, Televised Message from the Gemelli Hospital to the Eucharistic Congress, Lourdes, 21 July 1981.
16. Vatican II, Liturgy Constitution, 8.
17. *Lumen Gentium*, 7.

It is from the Eucharist that all of us receive the grace and strength for daily living – to live real Christian lives, in the joy of knowing that God loves us, that Christ died for us, and that the Holy Spirit lives in us.

Our full participation in the Eucharist is the real source of the Christian spirit that we wish to see in our personal lives and in all aspects of society.

We are able to love one another as Christ loves us only because his Spirit lives in us. In Baptism and Confirmation, we are united to Christ and filled with his Spirit. In the sacrament of the Eucharist, his Body which was given for us and his Blood which was shed for us, become the source of our strength.

His victory over sin and death, the source of our freedom, our joy, our eternal glory, is already within us. We receive the Body, now glorious, as the pledge, the beginning, of our own glory. If we receive it properly, the Eucharist transforms our lives; it 'helps love to triumph in us – love over hatred, zeal over indifference'.

Did not our hearts burn within us? (v. 32)

A change of heart is the beginning of the transformation of our lives. That change comes in response to listening to the word of God and welcoming it.

The word of God, which created the universe, summoned a people, 'Israel whom I have called' (Is 48:12). God revealed himself to his people in words and deeds. By listening to his voice they could 'understand his ways more fully and more clearly and make them more widely known'.[18] Because his people were, and are, sinful, the word of God is a call to change, to repent:

> You have neither listened nor inclined your ears to hear, although the LORD persistently sent to you all his servants the prophets, saying, 'Turn now, every one of you, from his evil way and wrong doings, and dwell upon the land which

---

18. Vatican II, *Dei Verbum*, 14.

the LORD has given to you and your fathers from old and for ever; do not go after other gods to serve and worship them, or provoke me to anger with the work of your hands. Then I will do on to you no harm.' (Jer 25:4-6, REVISED STANDARD VERSION).

In Christ, the Word of God takes flesh and dwells among us, like us in all things but sin. 'Jesus began his preaching with the message, "Repent, for the kingdom of heaven is close at hand"' (Mt 4:17). The disciples on the road to Emmaus felt their hearts burning within them as the Word of God himself explained the Scriptures to them. Their hearts burned because their foolishness and slowness of heart were being broken down and because the realisation that the kingdom of heaven was close at hand was drawing them to repentance and to the joy of salvation.

In the Mass, we walk with the disciples on the road, listening to the Lord. 'Christ is present in his word since it is he himself who speaks when the Scriptures are read in the Church.'[19]

In the Liturgy of the Word, God still speaks to his people, to gather us to himself, to help us to understand more clearly, to show us the need for a change of heart. Listening to the word of God we can discover who we are and who we are called to be:

> Such is the force and power of the word of God that it can serve the Church as her support and vigour, and the children of the Church as strength for their faith, food for the soul, and a pure and lasting fount of spiritual life. Scripture verifies in the most perfect way the words: 'The Word of God is living and active' (Heb 4:12), and 'is able to build you up and to give you the inheritance among all those who are sanctified' (Acts 20:32).[20]

---

19. Vatican II, *Sacrosanctum Concilium*, 7.
20. Vatican II, *Dei Verbum*, 21.

We hear the words and are reminded of the deeds by which God in the *past* gathered his people of the Old and New Testaments. We say, sometimes a little superficially, that 'we are the Church'. The word of God makes it clear to us that the Church to which we belong is a living tradition with its roots in the world of Abraham and Moses and founded on Christ and his apostles; and it is a Church which is meant for people of every race and language and culture.

The word of God can illuminate and transform our *present* situation just as it did for the disciples on the road. The words of Jesus in Nazareth, if we have ears to hear, are always true: 'This text is being fulfilled today even as you listen' (Lk 4:21). When Christ speaks in the Scriptures read at Mass, he is speaking to each of the people gathered there and addressing their present lives: 'From [the Holy Scriptures] you can learn the wisdom that leads to salvation through faith in Jesus Christ. All Scripture is inspired by God and can profitably be used for teaching, for refuting error, for guiding people's lives and teaching them to be holy' (2 Tim 3:15, 16).

The word of God is a word of promise. It summons us to prepare for our *future* destiny, for 'the coming of our Lord Jesus Christ and how we shall all be gathered round him' (2 Thess 2:1). We are a people destined for eternal joy in the contemplation of God who reveals himself to us. That revelation already takes place in his creative word which brings all things into existence, in his saving word which gathers his people to himself, in his incarnate Word which opens the way to the final revelation in which 'we shall be like God because we shall see him as he really is' (1 Jn 3:2).

The word of God, which speaks to us in the liturgy, shows us our identity, our present challenge and our hope as the people whom he has called. We are encouraged, challenged, summoned to respond and aroused to a longing for our own salvation and that of the world:

In the readings, as explained by the homily, God speaks to his people, opening up to them the mystery of redemption and salvation, and offering them spiritual nourishment; and Christ himself is present in the midst of the faithful through his word. By their silence and singing the people make God's word their own, and they also affirm their adherence to it by means of the Profession of Faith. Finally, having been nourished by it, they pour out their petitions in the Prayer of the Faithful for the needs of the entire Church and for the salvation of the whole world.[21]

When Pope John Paul spoke to the seminarians in Maynooth, he reminded them that their entire lives and ministry should be based on the word of God. That reminder is true for Christians whatever their calling:

> The word of God is the great treasure of your lives. Through the word of God you will come to a deep knowledge of the mystery of Jesus Christ, Son of God and Son of Mary: Jesus Christ, the high priest of the New Testament and the Saviour of the World.[22]

If we allow our hearts to be touched by the word of God at Mass, we are walking not just with the disciples on the road to Emmaus, but with Mary the Mother of God, 'the first of "those who hear the word of God and do it"'.[23] With her, we recognise that this is not a word to be heard and forgotten (Jas 1:23), but to be treasured and pondered in our hearts (Lk 2:19).

The one to set Israel free (v. 21)

The saviour of the world was called Jesus because he was 'the one who is to save his people from their sins' (Mt 1:21). The full

---

21. *General Instruction on the Roman Missal*, 55.
22. John Paul II, Address to seminarians, Maynooth, 1 October 1979.
23. John Paul II, *Redemptoris Mater*, 20.

setting free of human beings can be found only 'in communion with their God'.[24] We are created by him and for him and can never be happy apart from him.

The love expressed in the broken Body and the Blood poured out is a totally undeserved offer of friendship from the infinite God to the creatures he called into being. It is an offer of fulfilment that we could never have imagined if God had not first loved us.

But that is not all. It is an offer of forgiveness to creatures who have repeatedly spurned the Creator's gift of his love. We are creatures of a God so infinite in love that he continues to love even when a being that he made out of nothing rejects him:

> It is precisely because sin exists in the world ... that God who 'is love' cannot reveal himself otherwise than as mercy ... Infinite are the readiness and power of forgiveness which flow continually from the marvellous value of the sacrifice of the Son. No human sin can prevail over this power or can limit it ... Only a lack of good will can limit it, a lack of readiness to be converted and to repent.[25]

The forgiveness of God that is offered in the sacrament of Penance 'comes to us through the merits of [Christ's] death – the very death that we celebrate in the Eucharist'. His Blood is shed for us 'so that sins may be forgiven'.

This is why there is a close link between the Eucharist and the sacrament of Penance: 'The Christ who calls us to the Eucharistic banquet is always the same Christ who exhorts us to penance and repeats his "Repent". Without his constant, ever-renewed endeavour for conversion, partaking of the Eucharist would lack its full redeeming effectiveness ...'[26]

---

24. Congregation for the Doctrine of the Faith, *Instruction on Christian Freedom and Liberation* (1986), 44.
25. John Paul II, *Dives in Misericordia*, 13.
26. *Redemptor Hominis*, 20.

This is also why it is appropriate that, at the very beginning of the Mass, as we gather in the Body of Christ to meet him in Word and Sacrament, our first act is to try to answer his call to repentance and to recognise our need of God's merciful love. The unlimited self-giving of Christ, which we celebrate in the Eucharist, gives rise in us, with all of our limitations, 'to the need to turn to God in an ever more mature way and with a constant, ever more profound conversion'.[27]

Sin is revealed in its true colours not so much by fear but by love. It is the unfailing, unwavering love of God that makes offences against him so shameful. The litanies in the third form of the Penitential Rite set the tone. They speak of Christ healing, calling, gathering, strengthening, reconciling, bringing peace, consolation, light, food, forgiveness and life. We come to meet the Lord whom we have failed, but who *still* offers us his love and whose broken Body and spilt Blood are still offered for our salvation.

In the Mass, we celebrate the 'new bond of love so tight that it can never be undone', which was forged by that merciful love.[28] Once that love has been received, it becomes an inescapable duty to share it with others and with the world. It is one of the principal duties of the Church and of its members:

> ... to proclaim and to introduce into life the mystery of mercy, supremely revealed in Jesus Christ. Not only for the Church herself as the community of believers but also in a certain sense for all humanity, this mystery is the source of a life different from the life that can be built by human effort.[29]

Without forgiveness the world is doomed to be a place, at best, of cold justice, of irreconcilable claims, of oppression and of permanent strife.[30] The Lamb of God takes away the sins of the

---

27. Ibid.
28. Eucharistic Prayer for Reconciliation I.
29. *Dives in Misericordia*, 14.
30. Cf. *Dives in Misericordia*, 14.

world; those who are called to the supper of the Lamb should be examples of forgiving love: 'The Lord has forgiven you, now you must do the same' (Col 3:13).

The Church's role is 'to give a soul to modern society'.[31] Whether that is in bringing reconciliation to families, or hope to young people, or peace to our country, or social love and a sense of solidarity of the whole human family to the world, the key to that role is to proclaim and to live the mystery of mercy and forgiveness: 'Forgiveness demonstrates the presence in the world of the love which is more powerful than sin.'[32]

It is possible to see, in this light, why the sign of peace before the reception of Holy Communion is far from being a distraction. It is a sign that the love we receive is a love that we are called to share with neighbours and friends, with those we do not particularly like and, indeed, with complete strangers. The love which we celebrate in the Eucharist is a love which it is our duty to bring to the whole world. We should be able to begin by indicating that we rejoice in sharing God's merciful love with whoever is beside us in the Eucharistic assembly. What we share is not just our friendship and our good will. We are invited to share the *peace of Christ*. We join in giving thanks for that gift which we receive together.

The Eucharist, Pope John Paul told us in Dublin, is a call to look 'to the well-being of our families, our young people, our country, Europe and the world.'

He went to stay with them (v. 29)

The Eucharist is a Presence-Sacrament.[33] In a world that often seems to be marked by influences and situations in which the truth of Christ appears to play no part, the Eucharist is the guarantee and the reality of his presence.

---

31. John Paul II, Address to Conference of European Bishops'Conferences, 1985.
32. *Dives in Misericordia*, 14.
33. *Redemptor Hominis*, 20.

He is, of course, present in his word, in his Body, the Church, in the world which was made through him (Jn 1:2). But in the Blessed Sacrament we have 'his real presence in the fullest sense'. The Eucharist in the Mass and outside of the Mass is the Body and Blood of Jesus Christ, and is therefore deserving of the worship that is given to the living God, and to him alone.

In the celebration of Mass, we are in real contact with Jesus Christ in his death and resurrection. It is no mere reminder or re-enactment. In the Eucharist, 'the victory and triumph of his death are again made present'.[34]

We carry our daily lives into the Eucharist, into the really present triumph of Christ's death and rising to the glory of the new creation. At Mass, we offer every corner and every aspect of our lives with Christ to his Father. In doing so, we test them against Christ's love: we seek to see every part of our lives in terms of God's plan, as places where he comes to meet us; we try to discover what he wants of us, even in the most unlikely corners, because he is the Lord of our whole lives.

When we leave the church after Mass, we should be returning to lives that have become less materialistic, more penetrated by the awareness of Christ's presence, more closely united to Christ's self-offering. We carry the presence of Christ out into our daily lives not as something to be merely protected and preserved but as a richer inspiration and vision and as a source of strength in seeking to make life more Christian. Our recognition of Christ in the breaking of bread, in the Eucharistic celebration, should lead us to recognise him more clearly in the whole of life.

In particular, we should carry with us into the rest of life an awareness of his continuing presence in our churches. He stays with us through that Real Presence, inviting us to acknowledge him as God-with-us.

When we come prayerfully into his presence, we place ourselves in touch with the most profound truth about ourselves – that he

---

34. Council of Trent, quoted in Vatican II, *Sacrosanctum Concilium*, 6.

is our life and that the life we have is hidden with Christ in God (Col 3:3). In prayer before the Blessed Sacrament, we can come to 'experience and fully understand' how precious that life is.[35]

When we come prayerfully into his presence we meet him who is 'invisible Head of the Church, the Redeemer of the world, the centre of all hearts'.[36] It follows that prayer before the tabernacle ought not to be self-centred but should include the whole of creation – which is the sphere of Christ's presence and activity. Worship of the Eucharist should give a strong impulse towards 'social love'. This phrase, used by Pope Paul in connection with Eucharistic devotion, was a constant theme of the writing and speeches of Pope John Paul and is strongly expressed by Pope Benedict:

> 'Worship' itself, Eucharistic communion, includes the reality both of being loved and of loving others in turn. A Eucharist which does not pass over into the concrete practice of love is intrinsically fragmented.[37]

Before the presence of Christ in the Eucharist, we are summoned to 'consider as our own the interests of the community, of the parish, of the entire Church, extending our charity to the whole world, because we know that everywhere there are members of Christ'.[38]

They recognised him (v. 31)

The fact that we live in a world with little place for reverence or for a sense of mystery creates particular difficulties. In other times and in other settings, the transition from daily life to worship was less stark. Prayer was intertwined with the lifestyle of rural Ireland, for instance, in a way which does not happen in a modern city.

---

35. Paul VI, *Mysterium Fidei*, 67.
36. *Mysterium Fidei*, 68.
37. Benedict XVI, *Deus Caritas Est*, 14.
38. *Mysterium Fidei*, 69.

It may be that, on occasion, it proves very difficult to make the transition so that people leave the church with their minds still racing and distracted, without ever having 'changed gear' at all.

The two disciples recognised Jesus only after a long preparation. They had walked the road discussing the events of his passion and death; they had heard the Lord explaining the Scriptures that were about himself. We, in contrast, often come to the church or to Mass with our minds far from the Passion of Christ and far from the message of the Scriptures.

The approach to the presence of Christ, either for a private visit or for a liturgical celebration, has always been marked by preparatory gestures which can help to make us ready to recognise him. The sign of the cross with holy water at the door of the church recalls our Baptism, by which we were first born to the life of Christ and became members of his Body. The genuflection acknowledges him and greets him as the Lord of all creation. All of this is part of turning our minds and our whole beings to him. The respect and the quiet reverence, even in our physical posture, which we try to maintain in his presence, is a recognition that his is our life: 'The life I now live in the flesh, I live by faith in the Son of God who loved me and gave himself for me' (Gal 2:20, RSV).

The fact that we live in a world which is not conducive to worship, and where there are not so many reminders of religious truth as in the past, makes it all the more important that we should try to focus our minds on the presence of Christ in the Eucharist, not just at Sunday Mass but frequently throughout the week.

The atmosphere of today may tend to make people a little embarrassed at any public acknowledgement of the Eucharist. One can understand that consideration for those who do not share our beliefs may lead to a reconsideration of the timing, or the route, or even the practicality of a Eucharistic procession through busy streets in some places. But nobody should be offended by a person making the sign of the cross when passing a church or by someone calling into the church for a brief prayer before Christ present in the Eucharist. These are important ways of keeping the truth of

Christ before our minds and carrying his presence with us into our lives. The practice of making an Act of Spiritual Communion, in other words of uniting oneself in prayer to the Eucharistic presence of Christ, when one cannot receive Communion or even visit a church, might profitably be renewed.

There are some fine prayers after Communion in the Irish tradition which could express these ideas, for instance:

> O God, you are love without limit and
>   mercy without measure.
> Your love led you to come to me and my
>   hope led me to receive you.
> I give you my body to be your Temple,
> my heart to be your Altar,
> my soul to be your Ciborium.
> Lord, sinless Lamb,
> merciful Redeemer,
> noble infant Jesus,
> cover me with your cloak,
> give me lodging in your heart,
> absorb me into your kingdom,
> heal me with your fragrance and love,
> give me new life by your death,
> hide me within your wounds,
> cleanse me in your blood,
> bind me to your love
> and make me fully pleasing, Lord,
>   according to your Sacred Heart.

When the Blessed John Paul called on us to steep ourselves in the truth that comes from Christ, he clearly meant that more was required than a weekly attendance at Mass. He was talking about a steeping of ourselves in a truth that fills our lives. Indeed, at the close of the Great Jubilee Year, he wrote of the danger of 'shallow prayer that would be unable to fill [people's] whole life'. It would, he said, leave them as 'Christians at risk'.[39] In that filling of our lives with Christ's truth, a constant awareness of his Eucharistic presence is an important element:

> ... I encourage you in the ... exercises of devotion that you have lovingly preserved for centuries, especially those in regard to the Blessed Sacrament. These acts of piety honour God and are useful for our Christian lives ... The visit to the Blessed Sacrament – so much a part of Ireland ... is a great treasure of the Catholic faith ... Benediction of the Blessed Sacrament, holy hours and Eucharistic processions are likewise precious elements of your heritage – in full accord with the teaching of the Second Vatican Council ... Every act of reverence, every genuflection that you make before the Blessed Sacrament, is important because it is an act of faith in Christ, an act of love for Christ. And every sign of the cross and gesture of respect made each time you pass a church is also an act of faith.

The presence of Christ, the Lord of the universe, in our churches is not something that should be taken for granted. It should give rise to awe, reverence and thanksgiving. If we feel that the Lord is absent from much of our lives, that we are alone and in darkness, may this not be because when he offers his presence to us in the Eucharist, we have not sufficiently steeped ourselves in his truth and love? 'Come to me,' he said, 'all you who labour and are overburdened, and I will give you rest' (Mt 11:29).

They set out that instant (v. 33)
The significance of the Eucharist is not exhausted by the change that it brings in our lives, or even by the graces that it brings to the Church. What is at stake is 'the transformation of the world in the spirit of the Gospel'.[40]

---

39. John Paul II, *Novo Millennio Ineunte*, 34.
40. John Paul II, Holy Thursday Message, 1989.

The Eucharist is a call to greater effort, 'looking to the well-being of our families, our young people, our country, Europe and the world'. The very word 'Mass' derives from the sending out of the congregation at the end of the celebration: *'Ite, missa est.'* It is a name which highlights the fact that the Mass is the source of a new way of life, a new calling, a new mission, which is to bring the Good News in word and action to the world. A number of new formulas have been provided at the end of Mass to highlight this important moment: 'Go and announce the Gospel of the Lord'; 'Go in peace, glorifying the Lord by your life.' We set out from the Eucharist like the Emmaus disciples, filled with the message of Easter.

When people take part in the Eucharist as the Second Vatican Council wished them to do – aware, actively engaged and enriched by their participation – they are steeped in the truth which comes from Christ and in the strength which he offers us through his Spirit. That truth and strength are not just for the individual, nor even for the whole Body of Christ; they are for the whole world.

The Bread of Life and the Cup of Salvation are his broken Body and his Blood poured out for us. But the Christ who is present in the Eucharist is risen to a life beyond suffering and death. The real meaning of the Eucharist for our world lies in the fact that we celebrate at the same time the agonised death and the glorious resurrection of our Saviour.

Suffering, injustice, cruelty and evil are not eliminated from our world, but we celebrate the transforming power which has shown that it can overcome all of them. The truth of Christ is the truth that the world needs; it is a truth that exceeds all that we are entitled to expect. It is a message of real freedom. To the poor, Christ proclaimed the Good News of salvation: 'to prisoners, freedom, and to the sorrowful of heart, joy'.[41] This is a whole new world, a whole new reality: 'For anyone who is in Christ, there is a new creation; the old creation is gone and now the new one is here. It is all God's work. It was God who reconciled us to himself

---

41. Eucharistic Prayer IV.

in Christ and gave us the work of handing on this reconciliation' (2 Cor 5:17-18).

The Church, and every individual member of the Church, has this mission. The whole Church, Vatican II told us, is missionary by its very nature.[42] It is entirely right that, having steeped ourselves in the truth which comes from Christ, we should be sent to the wider world bearing within us the truth for which it hungers, even if the hunger is often unrecognised.

In his message addressed to the participants of the Eucharistic Congress in Lourdes in 1981, Pope John Paul summed it up:

> If it is true that the Eucharist Christ makes his Body and Blood sacramentally present, as well as his sacrifice of the Cross and his power of resurrection, it is so that we may communicate there in fullness; not just in spirit but also sacramentally, in order to go to the source who is Christ, and then, in concrete life and history, to go to our very limits, neglecting nothing which depends on human effort.[43]

We are sent out from the Mass, not overwhelmed by scandals and disasters, not disheartened by the pervading materialism and consumerism, nor disorientated and rudderless in the face of new values and trends; we are sent out as people who are steeped in the truth that comes from Christ. That is a truth which is deeper and stronger, more human and more liberating than any other vision of life.

We are sent out as people who have been reminded that in our lives there are huge blind spots. We spend large parts of our lives in contexts and activities where the truth of Christ appears to make little impact. We are sent out to bring the truth we have celebrated into all these areas. That was what Pope John Paul said in the Phoenix Park:

---

42. Vatican II, *Ad Gentes*, 2 *et passim*.
43. Televised Message, 21 July 1981.

> Our full participation in the Eucharist is the real source of the Christian spirit that we wish to see in our personal lives and in all aspects of society. Whether we serve in politics, in the economic, cultural or scientific fields – no matter what our occupation is – the Eucharist is a challenge to our daily lives.

He also developed those themes during his homily two days later in Limerick.

Nearly a decade later he reminded the whole Church of the need for the active, committed presence of lay people in the world of education, in places of scientific and technological research, in areas of artistic creativity and so on. It is the responsibility of the Church, and especially of lay people, to bring the Good News to bear in order to renew the life and culture of fallen humanity, to counteract and remove error and to raise the morality of peoples: 'Since the work that awaits everyone in the vineyard of the Lord is so great there is no place for idleness.'[44]

In order to fulfil that mission of giving a soul to modern society, of bringing hope to a world that cries out for it, we need first to be steeped in the truth that comes from Christ and in the strength of his Spirit. It is especially in the Eucharist that these are given to us:

> The living bread and wine regenerate our lives; they make us eager to accomplish Christian works, and give us charity to restore the whole universe. The Eucharistic bread, once offered for us, is endlessly given up so that people, formerly separated from one another, but repeatedly summoned by God to unity, should discover a new love for God in themselves and a new link for the necessary communion of life among them.[45]

---

44. *Christifideles Laici*, 3. Cf. *Christifideles Laici*, 44.
45. John Paul II, Letter appointing Papal Legate to Eucharistic Congress, Lourdes 1981.